MARBLE MADNESS

MARBLE MADNESS

Amanda O'Neill

Cartoons by Chris Pavely

This is a Parragon Publishing Book

Parragon Publishing
Queen Street House
4 Queen Street
Bath BA1 1HE, UK

Copyright © Parragon 2001

Designed, produced and packaged by
Stonecastle Graphics Limited

Text by Amanda O'Neill
Cartoons by Chris Pavely
Edited by Philip de Ste. Croix
Designed by Sue Pressley and Paul Turner
Diagrams by Malcolm Porter

ISBN 0-75256-246-0

Printed in China

Disclaimer:

Marbles are great fun but safety is
very important.

Do not allow babies or young children
under five years old to play with
marbles as they may swallow them.

Keep marbles away from family pets,
they could swallow one and choke.

Marbles must never be put in your
mouth or thrown about as they may
cause damage or injury.

Do not leave marbles where others
might step on them.

Always put your marbles away tidily
and safely.

The publisher and their agents cannot
accept liability for any loss, damage
or injury caused.

Contents

Introduction 6
The History of Marbles 8
Making Marbles 10
The Games 12
The Gear 14
Techniques 16
Rules of the Game 18

Archboard	20	Forts	32	Picking Plums	46
Bomber	22	Golf	33	Poison Ring	47
Bounce Eye	23	Handers	34	Potsies	48
Black Snake	24	Handspan	35	Pyramid	49
Bull's Eye	25	Hundreds	36	Ringer	50
Conqueror	26	Knuckle Box	37	Ring Taw	52
Crackers	27	Increase Pound	38	Spangy	53
Croquet	28	Lagout	40	Spanners	54
Die Shot	29	Lawn Bowling	41	String of Beads	55
Dobblers	30	Long Taw	42	Three Holes	56
Dropsies	31	Newark Killer	44	Tic-Tac-Toe	57
		One Step	45		

Games Needing Special Equipment

Solitaire 58
Bagatelle 60
Chinese Checkers 62

Introduction

Marbles are often miniature works of art. We take them for granted because they are so common, but some of them are real masterpieces of glassworking.

Whether machine-made or hand-crafted, it takes complex craftsmanship to produce their brilliant colors and varied patterns and you can find out how it's done on pages 10-11.

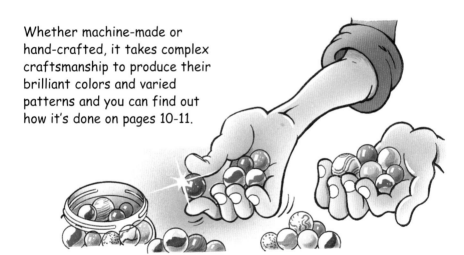

During the past 40 years, collectors have begun to appreciate marbles. Particular types are especially valued for their beauty, or their scarcity. A few glassworkers still produce hand-made marbles, every one different, mainly for collectors. Old marbles are often sought after – but watch out, for the market includes repaired specimens, replicas, and even fakes!

You may also get bitten by the collecting bug, but what marbles are really for is playing games. You can play marbles almost anywhere, on sidewalk or carpet, in a carefully measured tournament ring or a school playground.

In the days before cars and school buses, children used to liven up the walk to school with a game they called Plunkers, rolling marbles ahead of them as they walked and pocketing any that they hit.

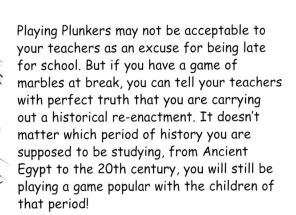

Playing Plunkers may not be acceptable to your teachers as an excuse for being late for school. But if you have a game of marbles at break, you can tell your teachers with perfect truth that you are carrying out a historical re-enactment. It doesn't matter which period of history you are supposed to be studying, from Ancient Egypt to the 20th century, you will still be playing a game popular with the children of that period!

The History of Marbles

Children played marbles in Ancient Egypt as long ago as 4000 BC, and the game has never fallen out of fashion since.

The very first marbles were made of baked clay, or of stone (sometimes marble stone, which probably gave them their name). Sometimes children used nuts, or cherry pits, or even knucklebones instead.

The glass marbles which are most popular today first appeared in Venice, home of great glassworkers, in around AD 900.

But making them was a slow, skilled job, so they remained rare and expensive. Clay and pot marbles were the standard kind for the next nine centuries.

In the 19th century, German factories started producing marbles on a large scale; they were made of both china and of a hard stone called agate. Agate marbles became so popular that stone marbles are still known as "aggies." America imported large numbers of German marbles, and then started manufacturing its own. By the 1840s one Ohio factory was producing around 100,000 clay marbles a day. Clay marbles were nicknamed "commies" or "commoneys" because they were so common.

In 1846 a German glassblower invented a gadget called marble scissors. This made mass production of glass marbles possible. Produced in many colors and elaborate patterns, they became highly popular in both the USA and the UK. By the end of the 19th century, machines for making glass marbles had also been introduced.

World War I hit marble production in Europe, and the US took over as the center of production. In 1922 the USA's first national Ringer tournament was held in New Jersey. Gradually mechanization of marble-making increased; in 1925 a method of machine-feeding three colors for swirls was developed.

In the 1950s Japanese cat's eye marbles became popular. Today most machine-made marbles are produced in Asia and Mexico. A few studios still produce hand-made glass marbles for collectors.

Making Marbles

So how do you make a marble? Most marbles are made in glass-making factories. It's a useful way of using up scrap glass – left over from the manufacture of larger glassware. This is melted down in a glass furnace, at a very high temperature, and colored as required with various oxides.

The melted glass is poured through marble-sized holes. A simple stream of glass is used to make marbles of a single color. For marbles with patterns inside, thinner streams of differently colored glass can be fed into the center of the main flow.

The flowing glass is already cooling and beginning to set, but is still soft enough to be snipped into marble-sized bits by machine-operated shears. These bits pass on to mechanical rollers which shape them into round balls.

Hot glass has to cool down very gradually, or it will crack. So the balls of glass pass on to a heated oven called an annealer, where the temperature drops slowly to room temperature. And there you have your marbles!

A very few glass studios still make marbles by hand, employing the same techniques used for centuries. The marble artist picks up melted glass on a metal rod and rolls it into a long glass cylinder. Hand-made marbles give the glassworker a chance to show off his skills.

PUNTY MARKS

Hand-made marbles have a little mark, called a punty, at each end where they were cut from the original glass rod that is called a punty. In some old marbles the punty is quite rough, but often it was ground down to leave a smooth facet.

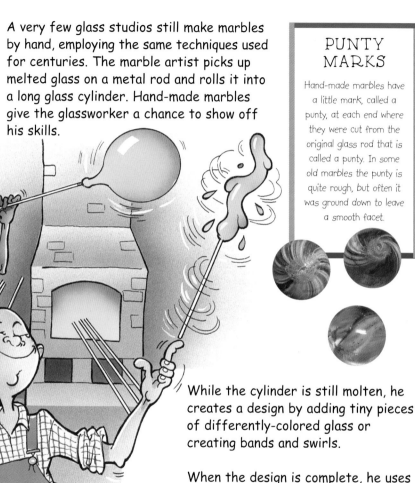

While the cylinder is still molten, he creates a design by adding tiny pieces of differently-colored glass or creating bands and swirls.

When the design is complete, he uses special shears to cut the cylinder into marble-sized pieces, which are shaped with hand tools and finally smoothed off with a blowtorch. The results are miniature masterpieces.

The Games

Nobody knows which games the Ancient Egyptians or the Romans played with their marbles. In fact, nobody knows which games were played even in much more recent times, because they were never written down.

We do know that some of the games in this book, like Ring Taw and Increase Pound, have been played for more than a hundred years.

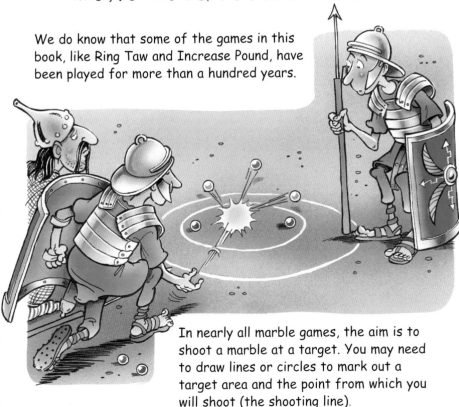

In nearly all marble games, the aim is to shoot a marble at a target. You may need to draw lines or circles to mark out a target area and the point from which you will shoot (the shooting line).

For some games, you scrape shallow holes in the ground as targets, while for others you use natural lumps and bumps in the ground to add to the challenge. You can also make special targets, like the arches of Archboard and the wickets of Croquet. Games like Golf and Croquet are small-scale versions of larger sports.

Marble games can be as simple, or as complicated, as you like. Most of the games in this book are for two or more players, but some two-player games, like Hundreds, are included. If you're stuck, you can even play a simple game like Lagout on your own.

The Gear

When it comes to the crunch, the only essentials for playing marbles are a playing surface, and a handful of marbles. If you also have a stick of chalk to mark out your target and shooting lines on a paved or concrete surface, you have all you need for most of the games in this book.

Smooth, hard surfaces like concrete make the easiest playing areas. But few surfaces are unusable – even bumpy paths or grass lawns can be pressed into service.

Still, if you want to be sure of a good surface, it's worth taking a little time to make yourself a marble mat.

A marble mat is simply a piece of fabric which you can lay down to play on. You need a piece measuring about 10ft by 10ft (3m by 3m) – an old sheet, a tablecloth, or a lightweight tarpaulin will do. If you mark out a series of circles on this with a felt pen, you will have your target areas prepared ready for a whole range of games.

To draw the circles, you need a piece of string about 6ft (180cm) long, a tape measure, a felt pen, a nail or pin – and a friend to help you.

Fold the sheet in quarters to find the center of it, and mark this spot. Fix one end of the string to it with the nail, and get your friend to hold it firmly in place. Tie your felt pen to the string at a point 5ft (1.5m) from the nail. While your friend steadies the nail at the center, pull the string tight and run the felt pen round the fabric to mark out a circle.

Shorten the string to 4ft (120cm) from center to pen to draw a second circle. Repeat with a 3ft (90cm) length of string, then 2ft (60cm), 18in (45cm), 1ft (30cm) and 6in (15cm).

Now you have seven circles, 10ft (300cm), 8ft (240cm), 6ft (180cm), 4ft (120cm), 3ft (90cm), 2ft (60cm) and 1ft (30cm) across. Draw a cross in the center of the circles, extending across the four innermost rings. And there you are, with target areas ready marked out for a wide range of games, on a smooth, portable surface.

Techniques

Some games need very little in the way of technique: you can just throw your marbles as suits you best. But for most games it helps if you develop a bit more skill. Here are four basic methods to try.

FLICKING

Place a marble on the ground, and set the tip of your thumb just behind it. Bend your forefinger so that its first joint rests on the first thumb joint. Now flick your forefinger forward so that it strikes the marble. This method launches your marble fast and hard – accuracy takes practice!

FULKING

This is a very similar method, with thumb and forefinger swapping roles. Place the knuckle of your forefinger on the ground, and balance your marble in the bent forefinger. Now put your thumb behind the forefinger and flick the marble forward.

KNUCKLING DOWN

Position your marble as for fulking, but this time place your thumb to the side of your finger, toward the palm. Use your thumb to launch the marble sideways from your finger, keeping your knuckles steady on the ground.

BOWLING

With the back of your fingers touching the ground, hold the marble in your palm and roll it toward the target.

Rules of the Game

Each game has its own rules, but it's a good idea to agree some general rules before starting play.

These might include:
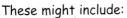
- Are you playing "keepsies" (players to keep any marbles they win) or "fairsies" (players to hand back marbles at the end of the game)?

- What happens if the playing surface is disturbed? Other children or the family dog may charge through the middle of the game, sending marbles flying.

- What happens if the game is interrupted? Parents or teachers are liable to call you away at the most awkward moments.

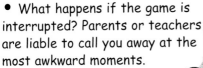

TARGETS AND TAWS

Marble players have a language of their own. In fact, they have several, with different words used in different regions, or the words used vary over the country.

For that reason, the only technical words used in this book are "Target" and "Taw."

Your target is, pretty obviously, the marble you aim at. Your taw is the marble with which you aim, sometimes known as your shooter.

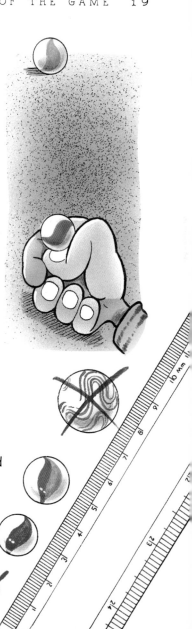

TYPES OF MARBLE USED

Marbles come in different sizes. The smaller the marble, the easier it is to aim. The very largest are usually kept for targets, or kept as collectibles.

Tournament games have strict rules on marble size: taws must be between 1/2in and 3/4in (13mm and 19mm), and targets 5/8in (16mm).

Marbles under 1/2in (13mm) (known as peewees) and over 3/4in (19mm) (known as bumboozers) are barred from tournaments.

Archboard

There are many versions of this game, which is also known as "Bridges," "Bridgeboard," or "Nine Holes." For all of them, you need a piece of cardboard with several (let us say nine) holes or arches cut into the bottom edge.

The easiest way to make your arches is to cut them into the long edge of a shoebox. Make them different widths, so long as each is wide enough for a marble to roll through it.

Number the arches from 1 to 9, giving the highest number to the one which is narrowest (and therefore hardest to score in).

One player is chosen to be keeper of the arch. The others take turns to shoot at the arches from a shooting line 6ft (150cm) away.

If your taw goes through an arch, the keeper must pay you the number of marbles indicated by the number of that arch. If you miss, the keeper wins your taw.

After an agreed number of rounds, another player takes a turn as keeper of the arch.

TALKING OF ALLEYS

If something suits your tastes, we say, "It's just up your street," or "just up your alley."

But in 1920s slang, people said, "That's just my alley-marble" – alleys being the best kind of marbles used in games.

Over the years, speakers mixed up marble alleys with the kind of alley you walk along!

VARIATIONS

You can also play this game without a keeper. Instead, everyone puts an agreed number of marbles in the pot. Players then aim at an arch, and if successful collect the marked number of marbles from the pot. In another version, players keep score for every arch they score in, and add up their scores at the end. The player with the highest total wins the pot.

Bomber

This is a game for two players, and it has two parts.

In Part 1, Player 1 throws a marble any distance. This is the target. Player 2 bowls or tosses a taw at it. If the taw hits the target, or lands within a handspan of it, Player 2 keeps the target marble. If not, both players get their marbles back and start again.

After an agreed number of throws, the two players swap roles.

In Part 2, Player 1 throws a target marble again. This time Player 2 tries to "bomb" the target by dropping a marble on to it from eye level. (Bending down to get nearer is cheating, and you have to take the shot again.)

If the marble "bomb" hits, Player 1 wins the target marble: if it misses, Player 2 keeps it.

MARBLES AT WAR

In the late 18th century, naval ships often loaded their cannons with limestone marbles – cheaper than cannonballs! Later, during the American Civil War, the Union ship the *Essex* used a mixture of stone, pottery, and glass marbles in her cannons to attack a Confederate ship, the *Arkansas*.

Bounce Eye

Draw a circle 1ft (30cm) across on the ground.
Each player put the same number of
marbles in the circle.

Take it in turns to stand over the circle and drop a taw marble down into it from eye level. You win any marbles you manage to knock out of the circle. If you don't win anything, your taw joins the group of targets in the circle. When there are no marbles left in the circle, the game is over – and whoever has most marbles is the winner.

Black Snake

For this game you need to build an obstacle course.
Find seven different objects – such as a shoe, a book,
a plastic bottle, etc., and number them 1 to 7.
Now lay them out on your playing area.

Decide who plays first. Shoot your taw at obstacle Number 1 from 1ft (30cm) away. If you hit it, go on to aim at Number 2. You are allowed to move your taw one handspan away from the object you have hit. As soon as you miss one, your turn ends and the next player has a go. If you hit an object out of order, you have to start again.

If you have two successful turns hitting all seven objects, you become a "black snake." This means you can use your taw to hit other people's marbles off the course. If you hit an opponent's taw, that person is out of the game – unless you knock the taw into one of the obstacles, when you are out of the game.

Bull's Eye

Draw four circles, one inside the other. The innermost circle should be 1ft (30cm) across, the others 2ft (60cm), 3ft (90cm), and 4ft (120cm) across.

In each circle, write the number of points you win if a marble lands there, the inner circle earning the highest score – just as on a shooting target. Draw a shooting line 6ft (180cm) from the outer edge of the biggest circle. Decide how many rounds will make up the game.

Each player in turn stands on the shooting line and shoots three marbles at the target. Each marble that lands in a circle earns the number of points marked there. (Landing outside the circles scores nil.) Add up the points of all three marbles for the player's score. At the end of the turn, the marbles are picked up to leave the field clear for the next player.

When everyone has had a turn, start the next round, adding on the scores. The winner is the player with the highest total score at the end of the game.

Conqueror

You can play this game with between two and four players.

Decide who is going to play first. Then Player 1 throws a marble any (reasonable) distance. Player 2 aims a taw at it. A hit means that Player 2 wins the target marble, and throws a new target to restart the game. A miss means that the player's taw stays where it lands and becomes a second target.

BOUNCE ABOUT

This is played in the same way as Conqueror, but target marbles (known as "bouncers") are generally not forfeited. If a bouncer is hit, the owner pays the thrower one marble.

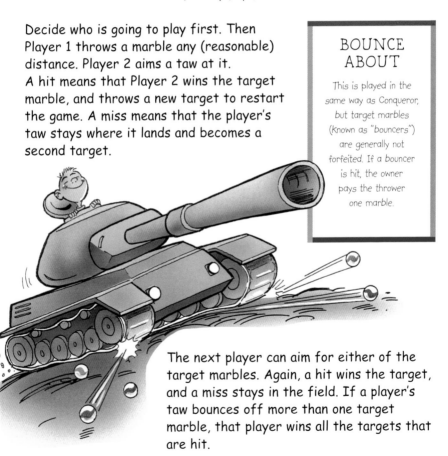

The next player can aim for either of the target marbles. Again, a hit wins the target, and a miss stays in the field. If a player's taw bounces off more than one target marble, that player wins all the targets that are hit.

Crackers

Also known as "Rockies," this is a game to play on rough paving, where there are plenty of cracks and rough edges.

One player becomes keeper of the marble, and places a target marble on the path in a position where it will be hard to hit. Players mark out a shooting line about 10ft (3m) from the target, and the keeper offers a number of marbles as the prize for hitting the target.

Players take turns to shoot at the target. Any taw that misses is forfeited to the keeper. The first person to hit the target wins the prize.

Croquet

For this four-player game, you need a set of nine hoops (or wickets). You can make these out of paper or polystyrene cups.

Cut the base off each cup, so that it forms a tube. Then cut each tube in half lengthwise, to make two long arched hoops.

Number the hoops from 1 to 9, then place them randomly around your playing area. (You may need to use masking tape to keep them in position.) Draw a shooting line 1ft (30cm) in front of hoop No. 1.

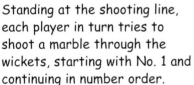

Standing at the shooting line, each player in turn tries to shoot a marble through the wickets, starting with No. 1 and continuing in number order.

A miss means the end of your turn. Leave your marble where it lands, and shoot from that position when your turn comes round. The first player to shoot successfully through all wickets in turn is the winner.

Die Shot

This is a marble game, a dice game, and a balancing trick all in one!

To start, you need to balance a die on top of a marble. If you are playing on a soft surface, push the marble a little way into the ground to stop it rolling around. On a hard surface, you need to use a marble with one surface slightly ground down to form a flat base.

MAKING MARBLES

Hand-made marbles are often made by cutting sections off a long cane of patterned glass and shaping them. But they can be made individually by winding melted glass on to a rod until a ball is formed, then decorating the surface with dots, stripes, etc. Each marble made this way is unique.

Players take it in turns to be keeper of the die. Other players in turn pay the keeper one marble to have a shot at the die from an agreed distance.

A player who knocks the die off the marble wins from the keeper marbles to the number shown on the face of the die. But if the player misses, the keeper wins the taw marble.

Dobblers

Draw two parallel lines on the ground, 3-4ft (90-120cm) apart.

The first line is your marble line. Each player puts the same number of marbles along it, leaving two finger spaces between marbles.

The second line is your shooting line. Stand behind it, and take turns to shoot a taw at the target marbles. You win any target that you hit. If you miss, your taw stays where it is and you take your next turn from that position.

If another player hits your taw, you must add another marble to the target line.

The winner is the player who has most marbles at the end of the game.

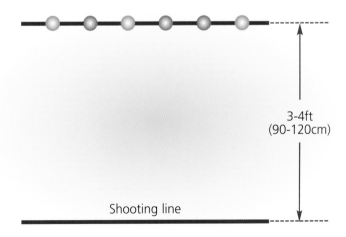

3-4ft
(90-120cm)

Shooting line

Dropsies

**Draw a 3ft (90cm) square.
Each player puts four or five
marbles in the square.**

Players stand with their feet outside the
square, and take turns dropping a marble
from waist height on to the marbles in
the square.

If you knock a target marble out
of the square, you win that marble.
Your turn continues as long as your
taw stays inside the square when
you hit another marble. If you
miss, or your taw rolls outside
the square, it's the next
player's turn.

The winner is the
first person to
knock five
marbles out
of the square.

Forts

Draw four circles, one inside the other, making the smallest 2ft (60cm) across, the next 4ft (120cm), the next 6ft (180cm), and the outer one 8ft (240cm) across. The inner circle is the fort.

Each player puts one marble in the outer circle, two in the next, three in the next, and four in the fort. These are the targets.

Players stand 2ft (60cm) away from the outer circle's edge and take turns shooting at marbles in the outer ring. You have one shot per turn. If you hit a target, you win it. If you miss, or hit a marble in the wrong circle, add one marble to those in the fort.

If your taw lands in a circle, leave it there and take your next shot from that position. Hitting another player's taw instead of a target marble carries no penalty, but you don't win the taw.

Players go on taking turns until the outer circle is empty. Then you start on the next circle, and so on. In the third circle, a hit entitles you to a second throw, and when you reach the fort, two hits earn you a third throw.

The game ends when the fort is empty. The winner is the player with most marbles at the end of the game.

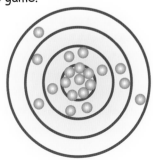

Golf

Dig out 18 shallow holes, lined up in a row, and number them from 1 to 18. Then draw a shooting line a short way away.

Each player puts the same number of marbles into the pot.

Take turns trying to shoot a marble into the first hole. If you miss, leave your shooter where it is for your next turn. If you succeed, you can go on to the next hole. Write down the number of turns you take to get your marble into the hole, keeping score for each hole.

At the end of the game, the person with the lowest score wins the marbles in the pot.

ROLLING STONES

Early marbles were often made of stone, particularly alabaster, agate (a kind of quartz), and limestone. The stone might be heated or dyed to create attractive colors.

Handers

This is a game of chance for several players.

Make a hole 3in (8cm) across, about 1ft (30cm) in front of a wall. Choose a spot to stand. From here, each player throws one marble at the hole to decide the order of play. The person whose marble is nearest the hole starts, followed by the person who comes second closest, and so on.

Each player gives two marbles to Player 1, who throws them all at the hole. Any that land in the hole are kept by the thrower. Any that miss remain in play and are handed to Player 2, who takes the next turn.

When all marbles are used up, a new round starts. Everyone contributes two marbles again, but this time the person who was Player 2 in the first round takes a turn as Player 1. This continues until everyone has had a turn as the first thrower of the round.

Handspan

This is a game for two players.

Draw a shooting line, and agree how many rounds you are going to play. In each round, one player rolls a marble any distance from the line to serve as target, and the second player shoots at it from behind the shooting line.

If your taw hits the target, or lands within a handspan of it, you have cleared that round and you keep your taw.

But if your taw ends up more than a handspan away from the target, you lose your taw to your opponent. (If one player has a bigger handspan than the other, you need to decide before you start play whose hand will be used for measuring!)

The winner is the player who has won most marbles at the end of the game.

Hundreds

This is a two-player game.

Draw a circle, or dig a shallow hole, about 1ft (30cm) across, and mark out a shooting line 10-15ft (3 to 4.5m) away.

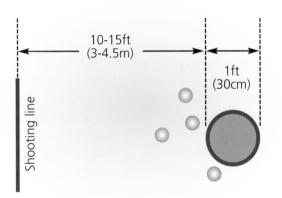

Shooting line

10-15ft
(3-4.5m)

1ft
(30cm)

AT THE END OF THE DAY

Glassblowers used to end their working day by turning glass leftovers into marbles for their children. These "end-of-day" marbles are usually large, and often wonderfully decorated with flecks and swirls of colored glass.

Players take turns to shoot a marble toward the circle. If your marble lands in the circle, you score 10 points and can shoot again. If it misses, retrieve your marble and let your opponent have a turn. The first player to score 100 points by getting 10 shots in the hole is the winner.

You can start this game by both of you shooting your marbles together. If both land in the circle, or both miss, both players retrieve their marbles and shoot again. The game only starts properly when one player rather than the other gets a marble in the circle, and then you continue as above.

Knuckle Box

Draw your box – a square measuring 2ft by 2ft (60cm by 60cm). Now draw a shooting line one handspan away from the box.

Scatter some marbles inside the box, at least four marbles per player, to serve as targets. Players take turns to shoot a taw from the shooting line, aiming to knock a target out of the box. Just to make it trickier, your taw must not roll out of the box itself.

You win any target marble you knock out, whether or not your taw remains in the box. If it does, your turn continues and you can have another shot from the shooting line. If it rolls out along with the target, your turn ends.

If you miss your target and your taw comes to rest outside the box, pick it up and wait for your next turn. But if you miss and your taw lands in the box, it stays there and becomes another target.

The game continues until the box is empty. The player who has won the most marbles is the winner.

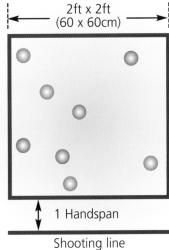

2ft x 2ft
(60 x 60cm)

1 Handspan

Shooting line

Increase Pound

Draw a circle 1ft (30cm) across. Around this, draw another circle 8ft (240cm) across.

The smaller circle is called the "pound," and the larger circle the "bar."

Each person contributes four or five marbles, which are scattered in the pound. Players take turns shooting at the targets from the bar.

If your taw knocks a target out of the pound and also comes to rest outside the pound itself, you win that target marble.

If your taw lands in the pound, you must put one marble into the pound before collecting your taw. If it lands outside the pound, but in the bar, it stays there and becomes another target.

If your taw lands outside both circles, for your next turn you can shoot from anywhere outside the bar.

If another player hits your taw, you must pay one marble to that player. The game ends when the pound is empty. The winner is the person with most marbles.

STEELIES

Factory workers used to bring home large ball bearings for their children to use as marbles. Known as "steelies," they make very satisfactory marbles for home play, but are banned in tournaments.

Lagout

Draw a line 2ft (60cm) away from a smooth wall.
Each player puts one marble on the line. Now draw a
shooting line 3ft (90cm) away from the first one.

Players take turns to shoot
from the outer line, aiming
to hit the wall so that the
taw rebounds to hit one of
the marbles on the target
line. The first player to
score a hit wins all the
marbles on the line. If your
taw misses, leave it where it
lands and on your next turn
shoot from this new position.

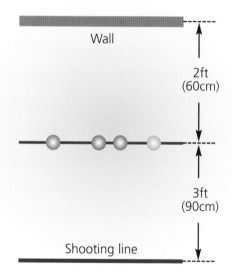

Wall

2ft
(60cm)

3ft
(90cm)

Shooting line

SPARKLERS

Some marbles have tiny
glittering specks of metal
inside – flakes of copper,
goldstone, or mica. These
may be scattered
randomly within the glass,
or arranged in bands.

In a simpler version of the game, each
player throws a marble at a smooth wall and
leaves it to lie wherever it rebounds. Now
players take turns throwing a marble at the
wall, aiming to bounce it off on to one of
the marbles on the ground. The first player
to hit another marble wins all the marbles
on the ground, and the game starts again.

Lawn Bowling

This is a game you can play on grass, or any rough ground.

Start by placing a large marble on the playing area.

Players take ten running steps away from this marble, in any direction. Now take turns to toss or bowl a taw at the target. Anyone who hits it wins automatically, and the next player has to put down a new target and the game starts again.

If no one scores a direct hit, the winner is the person whose marble is within a handspan of the target.

If no one comes within a handspan, any player whose taw is within 3ft (1m) of the target has another go by standing over the target and dropping a marble on to it from waist height.

If the target is hit, the next player puts down a new target; otherwise, the original target stays in place and everyone starts again.

Long Taw

This is a two-player game for long-distance shooters.

Draw a shooting line. At right angles from the center of the line, draw a target line 12ft (360cm) long.

At the center of the target line, 6ft (180cm) from the shooting line, place a marble. Your opponent places a marble at the end of the target line. Agree how many rounds you are going to play.

2nd marble

6ft (180cm)

1st marble

6ft (180cm)

Target line

Shooting line

PICTURE SHOW

Most marbles are plain-colored or patterned – but not all.

Rarities among older marbles include "Comics," with pictures of cartoon characters applied to the surface, "Sulfides," which have tiny clay models inserted inside clear glass, and china "Scenics," decorated with painted figures.

Take turns to shoot from behind the shooting line. Shoot first at the nearer target marble. If you hit it, you win it and go on to shoot at the farther one. If you hit that, you keep it as well and the round ends.

If you miss on either try, your taw stays where it landed and the next player takes a turn. This player can shoot at either of the targets or your taw. Hitting either target wins it and lets the player have another go; hitting your taw wins the player all the marbles.

A miss means that player's taw stays in the field and it is your turn again.

When there are no marbles left in the field, the round ends. For the next go, the player who started second on the previous round begins. Whoever wins the most rounds is the overall winner.

Newark Killer

Draw a small circle, with a shooting line 10ft (3m) away.

Each player needs ten marbles. Players take turns to stand behind the shooting line and try to shoot or roll a marble into the circle.

Each marble shot into the circle wins one point. If your marble is knocked out of the circle by another player, you lose a point: if it is knocked in, you gain a point.

When everyone has used all their marbles, whoever has most marbles in the circle becomes the "killer" and can shoot at any opponent's marble which is outside the circle. A hit means the killer keeps the marble and has another go. A miss means the game ends. The killer automatically wins the game.

One Step

Draw a marble line. Each player places the same number of marbles along the line, spaced two finger-widths apart.

Now draw a shooting line an agreed distance away. Players take turns to throw a taw at the target marbles. For your first turn, take one step forward before throwing your taw from a standing position. Later throws are made in the same way, but without taking a step.

MARBLES

Marbles were not called by their present name until the late 17th century. Until then they were known as "bowls" or "knickers" (from a Dutch word). No one really knows why we call them marbles. Alabaster marbles (the original "alleys") are made out of real marble, but most marbles are not.

You win any marble that is hit. Leave your taw where it lands, and start your next turn from that position. If your taw is hit by another player's taw, you must add one marble to the line. The winner is the player with the most marbles at the end of the game.

Picking Plums

This is a game for several players, who form two teams.

Draw a "plum line" 3-4ft (90-120cm) long, and shooting lines 3-6ft (90-180cm) away on either side of it. Each player puts in at least four marbles – you need a minimum of 16 marbles to start.

Divide into two teams, one to stand at each shooting line. Each team places their marbles, two finger-widths apart, along the side of the plum line which is farther from their shooting line. Now the "plums" are ready for picking!

The first team sends one player to have three shots from their shooting line at the other team's marbles. Any target marble knocked over the line is won by the shooting player's team. After each shot, the player retrieves his or her taw and any targets that it has won. (If you hit one of your own

team's marbles by mistake, replace it on the plum line.) After three shots, the second team puts in a player.

The first team to win all the others side's plums is the winner.

Poison Ring

Draw a circle 8-12in (20-30cm) across - the "poison ring". Around it, draw another circle 5ft (150cm) across.

Each player scatters three or four marbles within the poison ring.

Decide the order of play by each bowling a marble from outside the outer ring. Whoever lands a marble closest to the edge of the poison ring – but not inside it – shoots first.

The aim is to knock a marble out of the poison ring, leaving the taw inside the outer circle. If no target is hit, or the taw lands in the poison ring, you must put back any marbles won earlier in the game or, if you have no winnings, pay two marbles into the poison ring. A taw which lands in the poison ring stays there.

A successful shot wins the target marble. The taw that did the trick becomes "poisonous,"

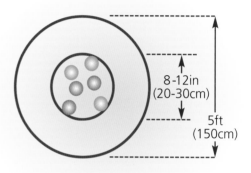

8-12in
(20-30cm)

5ft
(150cm)

and can be used next turn to shoot other players' taws. If it hits one, that taw is "poisoned," and its owner is out of the game. The "poisonous" taw keeps its powers until its owner has an unsuccessful shot.

The game ends either when the poison ring is empty, or when only one player is left – in which case that player wins all the marbles left in the poison ring. Whoever has most marbles at the end of the game is the winner.

Potsies

This is a game for two or three players.

Draw a circle 8ft (240cm) across. Each player puts the same number of marbles into the pot. Arrange them in a cross in the middle of the circle.

Players take turns to stand outside the ring and shoot at the target marbles. If you knock a target out of the ring, and your taw stays inside the ring, you win the target and can have another shot from your taw's new position.

However, if both the target and your taw end up outside the ring, the hit doesn't count. You have to replace the target where it was before, and the next player takes a turn.

The winner is the first person to win more marbles than he or she originally put into the pot.

Pyramid

Draw a 1ft (30cm) circle on the ground, and a shooting line 6ft (180cm) away. Choose who is to be keeper of the pyramid.

The keeper builds the pyramid in the center of the circle, using three marbles arranged in a triangle as the base and one balanced on top.

Players then pay the keeper a marble for each shot at the pyramid. The shooter wins any marbles knocked out of the ring. The keeper rebuilds the pyramid each time it is knocked down, using his or her own marbles.

When every player has had a turn shooting at the pyramid, change places so that the first shooter becomes the keeper for the next round. When every player has had a turn at being keeper, the winner is the person with most marbles.

Ringer

This is the official game played at marble tournaments.

Draw a circle 10ft (300cm) across, and draw a cross in its center. Place a marble at the center of the cross, and three more on each arm of the cross (making 13 marbles in total), spaced at 3in (7.5cm) intervals.

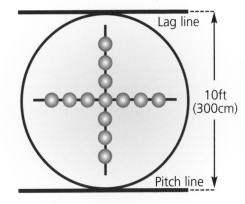

Lag line

10ft (300cm)

Pitch line

Draw a line on either side of the circle, just touching its edge. One is your lag line, the other your pitch line. To decide the order of play, each player shoots or tosses a marble from the pitch line to the lag line.

The one whose marble comes nearest the lag line (on either side of it) goes first, and the others follow in order.

For this game, you must use the knuckling down technique (see page 17). One knuckle must be touching the ground until your taw leaves your hand.

Players take turns to shoot a taw from outside the ring, aiming to knock a target marble out,

MARBLE MOB

On June 11, 2000, nearly 700 people gathered to play marbles at the Brooklyn Festival in New York, setting a new world record for the most people playing marbles at one time!

while making sure the taw stays inside the ring. If you miss, but your taw is in the ring, it stays there and becomes a target. If your taw rolls out of the ring you pick it up ready for your next turn, when you can shoot from any point on the ring line.

If you knock a marble or marbles out of the ring, hit an opponent's taw, or knock an opponent's taw out of the ring, your turn continues as long as your own taw stays in the ring. Once you miss, your turn ends and you add up your score.

The game ends when the ring is empty. You win any marbles you knock out of the ring. However, in Ringer it is usual to return all marbles to their original owners at the end of the game.

SCORING

Knocking a marble out of the ring scores one point and you win that marble. Hitting another player's taw without knocking it out of the ring also scores one point. The first player to get seven points wins.

Ring Taw

Draw two circles on the ground, the inner about 1ft (30cm) across, the outer about 7ft (2m) across. Each player puts an agreed number of marbles into the inner ring.

Decide the order of play. Players take turns to shoot a taw from any point on the outer ring at the marbles in the center.

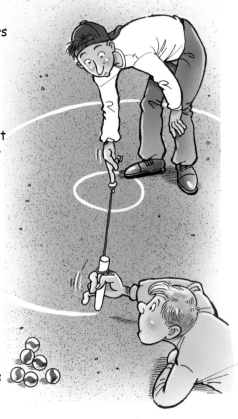

You win any marbles you knock out of the center, and can shoot again from the spot where your taw lies. If you miss, the next player takes a turn and your taw stays where it landed if it is within the outer ring. The next player can shoot at the center marbles or any players' taws that have landed in the outer ring. If he hits a taw, its owner has to pay him one taw and he gets another shot. The shooter may not strike the same opponent's taw twice in succession. The game continues until the ring is cleared.

Spangy

This game is for five players.

Draw a circle 10ft (3m) across, with a 1ft (30cm) square marked in the middle. Each of the five players contributes a target marble, one for each corner of the square and one in its center.

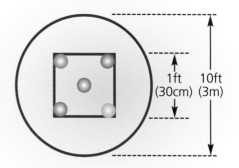

1ft (30cm) 10ft (3m)

Standing outside the edge of the circle, players take turns to shoot at the targets. If you hit one, you win that marble and can go on shooting. If you miss, that is the end of your turn and your taw stays where it landed to become another target.

GOLD IN THE GLASS

Coloring agents used for glass are usually oxides, such as cobalt oxide and zinc oxide. Some early glass marbles were colored by dropping a gold coin into the molten glass. The result, surprisingly, was pink.

If your taw lands within a handspan of any of the targets, you can try for a "spangy." Place your hand on the ground with your thumb next to your taw and your pinkie next to the target. Now close your hand in one quick movement. If you manage to knock the marbles together, you have won the target. If not, you lose your taw.

The game ends when there are no targets left in the square. The winner is the player who has won most marbles.

Spanners

This is a two-player game, and perhaps the simplest of all marble games.

One player throws a marble, which the other player shoots at. If you hit the target, or if your taw lands within a handspan of it, you win the target marble.

If you miss, your go ends and it is your turn to throw a marble for your partner to shoot at. When a player loses a marble, he or she must produce another or retire from the game.

String of Beads

Draw a circle 3-4ft (90-120cm) across, and another circle 8ft (240cm) around it.

Each player puts four or five marbles into the pot. Arrange these marbles round the edge of the inner circle, leaving even spaces between, like beads on a string.

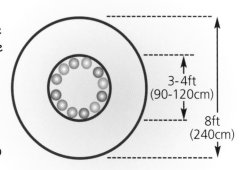

3-4ft
(90-120cm)

8ft
(240cm)

Players stand outside the outer circle and take turns to shoot at the target marbles.

GAS-POWERED COLORS

After 1920, marbles became brighter. New, brilliant, opaque colors appeared. The change was not due to new coloring agents, but to a change in the fuel used in the glass furnaces, from wood to gas.

If you knock a target out of its place, you win it. Your turn continues until you miss or shoot your taw out of the ring.

Leave your taw where it lands, and start your next turn from its new position. If you miss a target, you have to add a marble to the string of beads.

The game ends when all the marbles have been knocked from the string of beads.

The winner is the player who has won most marbles.

Three Holes

Make three shallow holes in the ground, about 3in (8cm) across and about 5ft (1.5m) apart, and number them 1 to 3. Draw a shooting line 5ft (1.5m) from the first hole.

Players take it in turns to shoot into each hole in order. If you miss, your taw stays where it lands until your next turn, when you shoot from the new position.

If your shot is successful and reaches the first hole, at your next turn you can go for the second hole – or you can choose to aim at any other players' taws which are lying in the field.

If you hit another taw, its owner must pay you one marble. When you have shot into all three holes successfully, each of the other players must pay you one marble. You can then start again at number 1.

Tic-Tac-Toe

In this two-player game, you each need five marbles which can be easily told apart from your partner's – for example, yours might be red while your partner's are blue.

Mark out a tic-tac-toe square, made up of nine inner squares, on the ground using a stick or chalk. Draw your shooting line 10ft (3m) away.

Players take turns to shoot marbles into the small squares, aiming to end up with a straight line of three marbles running up, along, or diagonally across three squares.

If your taw lands in a square, it stays there. If it misses, pick it up. If you land in a square which is already occupied by the other player's marble, you can only keep that place if your taw knocks the other taw out.

The winner is the first player to complete a three-marble line.

Solitaire

This name is also given to some kinds of single-handed card games (also known as "Patience") and to a board game played with pegs placed into holes.

To play Solitaire with marbles, you need a specially made wooden board with shallow cups into which the marbles are placed. Different types of boards are made. What is called the "British board" is circular in shape and has 33 cups. The "French board" has eight sides and 37 cups. When the board is set up for a game, every cup contains a marble.

There are two kinds of Solitaire game. In the most common, usually played on the "British board," the object is to clear the board leaving just one marble in play at the end of the game. You begin by removing one marble. Then you go on as in checkers, "taking" marbles and removing them from the board by jumping one marble over another into an empty cup. But "taking" moves differ from checkers in that they can only be made backwards, forwards, or sideways – not diagonally.

It looks easy, but unless you are very careful you will leave a few marbles stranded in positions where they cannot be taken.

The other kind of Solitaire is the "Pattern" game, usually played on the French board. The marbles are moved in the same way but are not taken from the board.

The aim is to make them form one of a number of traditional patterns. Some of these are simple, like the "E" and the "Cross." More complicated ones have such names as the "Apostles," the "Pirate" (or "Corsair"), and the "Globe."

DID YOU KNOW?

Solitaire (from the French word meaning "alone") is said to have been invented by a French nobleman held in solitary imprisonment during the French Revolution (1789-99).

Bagatelle

Even if you've never heard of this game, you'll know what it's about if you've ever played on an electronic pinball machine. In fact, it is sometimes called "pin ball," because it is played on a board studded with metal pins.

The board slopes toward the player at a shallow angle. On its right side is a "magazine:" a chute up which marbles (usually "steelies") are "fired" by pulling back and then releasing a spring plunger or by pushing them with a simple wooden tool. The marble runs up the chute and then gravity takes over, making it roll down the board.

Waiting for it are various sizes of cup-shaped "pens" formed by metal pins, and a few single cups rather like the holes on a putting green. A separate score is marked on each pen and hole. The larger the pen, the lower the score. And because it is much harder to get the marble into a single cup, these score highest of all. Single pins are deliberately sited on the board as additional hazards to deflect the marble away from the pens and cups.

The force with which the marble is fired is very important. A skilled player will fire a marble with just the right amount of force so that it glances gently off a single pin positioned at the very top of the board and runs gently down the center of the board, where it has the best chance of making a high score. If it is fired too gently, it may run back to the plunger and count as a "no-ball." Fire it too hard, and it may bounce over the higher-scoring places and reach the bottom of the board without scoring at all.

Usually, each player fires five or six marbles; the highest total score wins. There are many modern variations on the standard board. Some are "themed," with pictures and scoring spaces arranged so that the players can pretend to be astronauts navigating deep space or footballers scoring goals.

A simple version of bagatelle uses a board with no pens or cups. At its base is a "bridge" with eight or nine arches, each marked with a different score. The marble is fired in the usual way and runs down through a pin-maze which guides it at random to one or other of the arches. Here, winning depends on luck rather than skill.

A-MAZE-ING

You have probably played one of the hand-held maze games in which tiny "steelies" have to be maneuvered into cups by tilting the board to and fro in your hands. These developed in around 1890-1900, from an original model called "Pigs in Clover."

Chinese Checkers

Chinese checkers is probably the most attractive-looking of the board games that use marbles.

It is played on a board printed with a six-pointed star, and having 256 cups for marbles. Each point of the star is a different color, and each acts as base for an "army" of marbles of the same color.

Two to six people can play. In the two-player game, each

player's army consists of 15 marbles. The number is reduced to ten when four or more players compete.

The object of the game is to be the first to "march" your army of marbles across the board and occupy the opposite point of the star. As in Solitaire, the marbles are moved by jumping over one another into empty spaces. A player can only move one marble in his or her turn, in any direction. It can only be moved one step.

The idea is to take the right steps so as to put your marble in a position to jump over another – one of your own or your opponents' – into an empty square. If, after the first jump, you are in a position to make another, jumping continues until no more opportunities exist. This is like the multiple moves that you can make in a game of checkers. You cannot make both a step and a jump, or jumps, in the same turn.

The marbles that are jumped over are not taken off the board. In this game you are always playing for position, not destruction! Not only are you trying to go forward by jumping your opponents' marbles, you are also trying to position your own marbles so that they can jump over each other – and without offering "enemy" marbles an easy jumping route. You will find yourself dodging backward and forward across the board, wondering whether to move to advance your own marbles or block those of your opponents.

DID YOU KNOW?

Chinese Checkers, developed in the United States in the 1930s, is based on a British "war game" called Halma (from a Greek word meaning "a jump"), invented in around 1880 and played on a square board with counters or pegs.

Marble photographs supplied
courtesy of B. Alan Basinet
Alan's Marble Connection
www.marblealan.com
Email: Marblealan@aol.com

Useful address:

House of Marbles
The Old Pottery
Pottery Road
Bovey Tracey
Devon TQ13 9DS,
United Kingdom
www.houseofmarbles.com

The main supplier of marbles
in the UK, with branches in the
USA, France, and Germany, and
customers all over the world.
Also features a visitor center
and museum of marbles and
marble games in Devon, England.